Dale Jensen, in his wonderfully quirky book, Yew Nork, *proves himself a master of sound and sound's forms. In these adventuresome poems, the same-old ever-newness of meaning mirrors the repetitious yet uncaptured city. City, also, of the self, where the poet discovers the challenge of aging and the impossibility of reconstituting a past that, nevertheless, bullies and seduces the present. In* Yew Nork, *Jensen shows us not only how poetic form helps us to hear what is (literally) near, but how to use poetry's beat to reframe the (gone) past into what we want our present to be.*

— Grace Grafton, author of *Whimsy, Reticence & Laud, unruly sonnets*

Jensen's poetry gives us startling, energetic imagery that is funny, philosophical, mind-bending, poignant, and a bit frightening. A certain balance comes from absorbing his language and imagery that pours out of the subconscious to share the stage with the rational mind. There are so many lines and ideas throughout the poems in this collection that we should return to often in order to enhance/enlighten our own creative selves. What an opportunity to be 'stuck in a room with imagination like a top hat. . .' Yew Nork *is a mesmerizing, unforgettable, one-of-a-kind poetry collection.*

— John Rowe, author of *Winsome Lonesome* and president of Bay Area Poets' Coalition

Dale Jensen is the uncle of invention.

— Crag Hill, University of Oklahoma, author of *Another Switch* and editor of *Score* and *The Last Vispo Anthology: Visual Poetry 1998-2008.*

Dale Jensen's Yew Nork *is a bird's-eye view of a city that is, isn't, and was, wasn't. No Circle Line superficialities here but a poeta en nueva york registering, remembering, and imagining — lamenting 'it's no longer the house of fire i remember.' As the poet ages, his sympathies and his waistline widen, he shifts coasts but 'i stay on the same block for the rest of my life.' Selves keep showing up: 'that is i and i walking along.' It's a wonderful trip to 'the edge of old age' and 'the cool warm beast of my youth.' In this book, words hide within words and time runs backwards. But time can't run backwards: 'i remember meeting you several times that week / east tenth street and fourth avenue / your wave from against a wall / your voice asking for spare change . . . so this is how it probably is / to meet gods.'*

— Jack Foley, author of *Eyes* and *Visions & Affiliations, a California Literary Time Line* and host of "Cover to Cover," KPFA-FM.

5/9/15

FOR JEFF + ANNE,

IT's GOOD TO BE BACK.

Dale

Yew Nork

Poems by Dale Jensen

2014

Sugartown Publishing

Crockett, California

Yew Nork

ISBN: 978-0-9913870-3-8
LCCN: In Application

Sugartown Publishing
1164 Solano Ave., #140
Albany, CA 94706
www.sugartownpublishing.com
janniedres@att.net

Printed at Minuteman Press, Berkeley, CA

Cover art: courtesy of David Balmer, New York. *www.paulbalmer.com*

Book and cover design by Margaret Copeland, Terragrafix
Photo of author by Jannie M. Dresser

For Judy Wells

Table of Contents

Yew Nork

Armweary Traveler

the statue of liberty is much less impressive if people wear hats in front of you
those eyes that remember everything that happened
from the point of some choice that you made when you were twenty-two
you the platform   the laundry blesses you as it hangs across the torch
and there you stand wearing california around your neck like an amulet

it's strange having california hanging from my neck now
and it's so huge you can't move   speaking those accents
emotional threads wide as a treadmill obscuring every other direction
then you're big   you're supposed to choose
then disappear

the statue of liberty is much more impressed if you see it before it sees you
then she looks   then you think you're so small you're invisible
so you carry coney island around in your pants pocket for your last day here
she'll spend her life in thrall to that image
as you wave your torch in celebration and sink knee-deep in concrete

and the statue keeps staring   staring
and blessed are the subways   their clattered tempo slowing
to become your heartbeat
she's been my friend most of the time since i've been back
whatever of that beauty goes into your walk is worthwhile
you've made your choice   now you can't get out of the way
so please come back with me to my hotel room night doesn't set here
it made that decision when it first got out of college
the city's lights redefine night any time of the day
and any day still sits still just west across the water

Low Heat

men can survive without the slightest evidence
we live table   talk lazy   feeling new
constant temperature ambitious specks
of light we would have fulfilled

we down trenches   and in professional hope
by getting a little wounded
i could not picture shooting another drink at my expense
and rage when it stands trickier afterwards

    the insignificant angels
    the slightest change of plague-bound disgust
    the cauldrons of the stars unknown prospect of adventure
    a silly of all tears
    a tone of cold and perish
    you know it heats something   it cheated my fate

Puncture Wounds

you wonder who's been looking over your shoulder
when you realize that the toothmarks on your shoulder are yours

the wounds will have begun to fester
by the time you realize this

and how long that audible breathing
that sounds like it comes out of your lungs
but you swear is not your own
how long has that been going on?

why   is the reek
of that breath   so familiar?

don't say that it's coming past your ear
from behind you

right after that you notice
the necklace of teeth across your chest
and you wonder how those toothmarks
got all the way
to your shoulder

Union Square

as he got older as his years
got larger   a city larger within him

got fewer it got then a larger
city   then with skyscrapers
a basement   he got tall and fat
a basement   that reached to his voice

who is that old man
with a spine like a skyscraper
who complains about a gutache
or ulcers   or a spastic colon?
who is he?   why don't i
want to look at him
when i look   in the mirror?

i need to go to new york city
where the pulse runs like
it did when i was young

i need to see   and how i haven't
where there are so many
that are surprise   with their noise
that are both familiar and unfamiliar to me
the voice   of the city   i hear   at night
when all else is quiet   a sort of
unified hum   welcome me back
who i once was   to the air

Looking for Gods in Greenwich Village

i remember meeting you several times that week
east tenth street and fourth avenue
your wave from against a wall
your voice asking for spare change
the flood of new yorkness new to me
as the colors of your clothing   the colors of night
black and blue grey   charcoal
brown and an obfuscation of dust
that changed to its native form only
in nocturnal alleys a step from the realm
of streetlights and illumination

you were new york to me
new york beyond wealth and the glisten of rain
beyond museums concerts and organized noise
beyond what i understood as literature

you were bumming too
more deeply into your life than i was into mine
but in the same way our steps
trod between definitions
like those of centaurs on urban concrete

so this is how it probably is
to meet gods   the clarity of their form
their ambiguity without name or intersection
whole streets going back to before they were even
indian paths   and you know their stories even though
you'd never seen them then
never having really been there
as we looked at each other as a deer looks at a squirrel
each not thinking to imagine the other one
to be a mountain lion
or potentially one of the gods

Denly Ware

i hear them:

      sucks in abs o phorical saint
      munal soul just before it shakes hands with
      isolated   itted   denly aware of
      click   clack   prayed with after timing
      itself open in public   gument   glibly to say
      clear throat   rection   ar gue   think of myself now
      a self-delusion imagining itself in real time
      walk   walking's free   come on over ethereal meatball
           hot city at the base of the clouds

      newly seized power from its house of wart monkeys
      mermaids and sea elephants dunking green donuts
      in one of the side fountains where dren fidently play
      a biolinguistic image of a stewed dragon projected on a cathedral wall
      a kitten carrying a barrel of water in a coffee cup

Weight

after toDay at wORK
i FEeL Like the opPOsite Of coFfee

FATigue cOuLD reLAX you
but it gives YOU even MOre soLiD
weight BEtween THe AToms
of the PERSON THAT YOU WERE
FLOATING OFF to work this morning

as you Get OLDer
you get more SOLID

Watchdogs

even in front of rare rest the watchdogs
a drool start   hand-crawling what they are
a new york   of small decisions
all those little figures walking the skin
of an apple its own
leave the air to breathe
its own pollutions   its own natural
traffic jam of neural memory

       to see everything you've known to see
       born written in electrical fondness
       the minute that you close your eyes
       the view out the bus window
       all those faces   all that glass
       then open your eyes again

Walls

which performed would
i might be able to live here

when you're in trouble
you said tumbleweed

it's nearing midnight
they have blood walking
cramps erupt to plague and
i want to read you the
mistranslation of documents
circulation i hear you in my ears

facing the wall
i hear someone singing outside
the sound of the traffic in your wrist
the highway through the door in your hands

windows defining their own route
next place you go   say
i feel like i like it here
traintracks around the moon's
hat brim

Epaulet

i caught sight and was on my way
the building looked familiar appearing on doors and guys
zones of affluence and poverty   say
my old neighborhood never looked so prosperous

restaurant at then   too
store across the valley looking small crowds in their twenties
it's no longer the house of fire i remember
laundromat and a small motel asleep calling it lunch

    my consciousness is made up of storefronts
    i go to a different one every night   the haze
    seems static that way   i like to stay there
    i stay on the same block for the rest of my life
    buses go by about three blocks from here
    my passport crawls   up my sleeve to my shoulder

My Ripped Shirt

a herd of crabgrass
an elephant snake sneeze
a philosophy of parthenogenesis
from the collected giggle in your pocket
a collusion of laundromats
that the sneeze not be narrow
that its path be epic and tropical
that the word laugh be named specifically as law
and that your satchel be not named chicken soup
    no murinated mountebank minnesinger
    imaginary amphibian hitchhiker
    entanglements of the liberty of roadmaps
    open decanter of the dilemma of mixed certainties
    let me sneeze as cosmically as i want
log   fossil   cremation   blue star   octopus telegraph jibber jabber
conflagration of hot work bench sweat
sunset lawn chair of mouse and rat torsos
trepidation of false furs at the counter of dimestore truth
hilarious explosion of tea kettles at the last word of the gettysburg address
the crown princess' ruffles at the furthest edge of her dynasty's solar system
    these petroglyphs are written in english
    ants swimming in fossilized water
    you've been singing them since babyhood
    my ripped shirt is having an anxiety attack
flags wave wildest when wildflowered apes are waving them
into their armpits and declaring it everybody's national holiday
as fireworks invent themselves out of sawdust
and castle towers spurt glory openmouthed
excitement and lust are mere curves on your roadmap
their voice beyond idiocy
their truth beyond believing

Glance (for Kane's friend Bernstein)

can't see beyond the clouded
the walls like a career   remember
the couple i glanced on the subway today
walked the floors of an alternative universe
watched them like dust   the mud of an ulterior city
the same year   the same weather
the calm clarity of having been in love since college
bonded with the station i knew for that instant
     imagine them and their imaginary children
     envy them   even if you can't mention it
     imagine how she spoke   what she'd say to you
     saw her on the dock   never met her
     saw the ship leave and she was gone
     envy their life every day   if only its mystery

Beach

you should be careful around
the oceans inside your shoes

they can drown you

there is nothing to absorb them
even socks   even artificial sponge

they fill your shoes every time you walk
then   after you're used to that
they fill them every time you think
then your thoughts walk
carry you to the edge of an ocean
you couldn't have imagined otherwise

it's the loneliness there
the loneliness there that can drown you

Looking for Gods in Greenwich Village

i remember meeting you several hats in front of you
your voice asking for spare change across the torch
new york beyond wealth and the invisible

your wave from against a voice
that you made when you were twenty-two
that changed from its native form of treadmill
beyond what i understood as literal celebration
trod between definitions
east tenth street and your toothmarks
your voice asking will have begun to fester
in nocturnal alleys   your ear is not your own
that you notice teeth   before they notice you
that you were bumming
and it's coming past thrall to think that image

so this is how it got them larger
to meet gods   the with skyscrapers
whole streets going you've never seen an old man
then look in the mirror boy
each not thinking to be a mountain
as we looked at each ear of the city
i hear   at night
each not thinking is quiet
to be a mountain   welcome me back
or potentially one as to the air

After

so yesterday i envisioned headhunters
their tattooed hands and feet
my head is overflowing with art

three of them dressed in bear suits
maybe up near fortieth street
reading books about fences and borders

a feeling that they must seek out the wall
and the ocean of the sky
and the birds   how to talk to them

where my hunger isn't waiting
crouched like a demon in the cave of my stomach
waiting for the boats   the hints
that you can seek something that's really needed

the empty hurricane of the sky
the restrained bite and chew
of the paddles in the water

Month

it's when the blood
runs again in the tree
that the winter deities
born in snow
first hit adolescence

this happens every year
even though it's april only once
that's when it's first april
and after that april
april's only april again

i hate looking at myself naked in the mirror
october october   ha ha   october
it's really october and it's been october
for years and years now
i don't like the feeling
of getting used to this
october has thirty-one days to it

For Gotham Books

the feet of skyscrapers
the entire city its redness of eye
that is i and i walking along

the soul its own trophy
conversations between primitive brownstones
in the anonymity of midtown crowds

my surprise   then
when i saw you were gone
the space between buildings where you'd been
empty as the space of an extracted tooth

that you'd carried yourself away in good weather
that your city of my vision
was far from where you'd camped yourself
in the soul of another town

Evolution Poem

dinosaurs morphed into birds while on the wing
didn't land for centuries
finally   touched down
in the courtyard last night

where they had
no curiosity
at all
about the buildings
that had gone up without them

The Wind Seemed to Room (for my mother)

there was remember:
haunt gossip   up-thought
not a she wanted
she behaved enterprise
found his crib shaking babies
time babies
these last few moments she's mummy's boy
there had been no celebrated
     she pulled the soon
     she peered down into his doctor
     she knew what the house assured him
     she really put the wind   really seemed to room
     time ceased the moment she was certain
     you'll just have to be faces

Exchange

last night barry i saw you
walk past the glass walls of the diner
and in through the door as i talked with my boss
who excused himself as you and i
recognized each other

you still looked twenty-three
after these thirty-seven years
yellow shirt   brown jacket
cowboy hat and the hair still almost yellow
and delicate where it was bound in a ponytail

you nodded   got a coffee
sat at the table where the boss had sat
you were still twenty-three
clear skin clean eyes robust self-assurance
i was sixty and imagined myself desiccated

i couldn't imagine what to say to you
we used to talk for hours together
you sprawled and set your legs parallel to the table
played with your mustache and took another sip
been years   you said

here i was at the edge of old age and
what had i really accomplished since i was young?
here you were   still the age you were when we met
all future   all coolness   all good humor knowing that the gods
still held you as their darling

what could i say to you?   what could you say to me?
i finished my coffee and said i was due elsewhere
over due really   and you nodded and put your hat on the table
i said good to see you then walked out the door
you were still at the table   snow crunched under my feet

The Station

the cool warm beast of my youth keeps himself preserved
in a cold dark locker in the city inside my head
in the train station that disappears at dawn
with the blind automobiles of nighttime awareness
    i really feel lost without him
    as i walk the teeth of the bathroom floor
    that keep the bottoms of my feet awake

airplanes are asleep in my ears
and far under my feet is another city
where i would have wound up   brain awake
had i taken that last train i saw last night
before the streets turned to scattered marbles
and the cars shut down their lights and turned coward
    missing the train ride that continues this next morning
    along the long track
    that circles the sun and comes back to earth
    after a century of bright light and brilliance
    on its own genius journey   its own instant of eternity
    simultaneously on its start and its return
    to the beast that keeps all-night walkers awake
    in their stations of finite years and visible darkness
    in their stations of teeth cutting into footpads

Snow

i was stuck in a room with
imagination like a top hat
and across the street saw a bookstore i'd last seen
almost forty years ago on the other coast

      hello   i'd like to buy
      the snows of yesteryear
      i came all the way from medieval france for that
      and the guy behind the counter looks at me says
      did i know you in college?
      this bookstore was in toronto   anyway
      not the village or telegraph avenue
      i can hear cars like lungs
      passing behind his voice

and the glow   of winged bicycles on the wall
sometimes age needs wheels
i really want that book   i really do
i know the snow i've crunched through to get here
sometimes a street is just real enough
and you're on it

Pilgrimage

see it   wells hidden
parking lot is now a small childhood
no other place looked so strangely funny
rebuilt way to touchpad with reality
      i walked down
      all my current turmoil
            going through offended that it's
            so high up in an office building
                  the comforting child's hands
                  dreary drapes closed in a front window

kids grew up coffee in their energy hours
caught the bus to now until i
made it back alive   but still
      bought a shrine
      memory parked inside a gas station
            forced myself inside
            the glass of a window pane
            bone inside a reliquary
            in a shaky chapel for unbelievers

kids grew up coffee in a vacant lot
outside the cardboard fence surrounding the brides of a spanish mansion
hope landing live as a subway ride
inside the clouds that sway under the sea
      the past is a shell
      through sharp mouths
      of dog teeth
      you can never get used to

Two Kids Playing Catch

that once   as i was a kid
made no idea
the storm drain was much louder then
old age brings secrets of helicopters

to an older body   the black sky of sleep
at first draw a blue stripe at the top of the picture
the first time i went down to the subway
i hold its bones like dice in my hand

> behind grey clouds there is invisibility
> the water's at the lip of the cup now
> then there's green   that's grass   at the bottom
> people waiting hardly moving for the next train
> you'll never reach this age if you think about it
> so much space between green and blue

The Brilliant Delusion

next morning   the only hint of the flight face cards
the friend down the hall flew open for breakfast
an impulse that descended into the eternal fire
on the other side of the door   furnace of anyone
each car that goes by adds smoke to it

i used to like driving those things
well over one hand long
heat like weather   ace break
the face above the fireplace its smoke-heightened smile
mouth open the heat of his words the cool never betraying him

purely this one he'd pulled from mid-deck
it's less bad being young than not being yet
slack   furnace-jawed in adolescent memory
its shadow forming a coat of mink of the ash around him
     all now it's like a free fall from heaven
inhale their fumes wonder if his breath's been excluded
the adolescent lung pressure   middle-aged jailsuit breakdown
as each ash presses another hot year into fur
furnace door toothed and open
     i wonder what fire
     flames from the card
     he thinks he's drawn
this time

Pomp and Circumstance

i once thought of life as a play
one's own play
with one's seat center stage for the duration

but now i think that that isn't true
that one's life really is a play
that all the characters one knows are in it
that they are all in the play their entire lives
and   still   that one's one's own main character
but that that character is born and dies
in the middle of the third act

Stopping for a Look Inside

once a year the year rolls around again
its little prickly stabs of
but down the street the salvage place has plenty of bathtubs
its eighteenth century clockface   all the odd palaces
there are thorns on most of the limbs
every time the pendulum swings the crowd gasps in admiration
our old neighborhood is looking a little grungy these days
or at least wear thick gloves and a jacket with heavy sleeves
      the old hollywood club is stripped to its beams
      the bus goes past me as i look through its planked-over windows
      time is slowing down   i remember the
      times i walked past this place on my way to the burger joint
      nothing there i ever noticed except for music sometimes
      now it's empty   soundless like the inside of time

This Town that Glows

this town i see in my dreams
is a town of penthouses and subway stations
steel and glass houses glowing by night
lightning you can sense with your eyes closed

the women i dreamed of sleeping with in college
are all gathered in the college library
all in their teens and twenties   reading to each other
from the books that will be written by their grandchildren

      dreams in this town are things of fever
      demon lovers   their backs turned to the banality
      of the stolid background of the merely physical

      if they'd reappear as trains in the subway of my gut
      or confess to having loved me or even someone like me
      i could levitate in the night   through the unsighted emptiness

The Hangman's Beautiful Children

fishing for muses   here on the subway platform
for the hangman's beautiful children
full of wheel sharp of ankle
loose of blouse strap long of boot
and in her hands
tissue paper origami crane

bright of clothing even if her clothing's black
eye shadow with eye flash bright within it
sinuous deep animal stride
even in the routes of his fingertips
as they cross the keyboard of a laptop
screen depth of light that can shut off in an instant

o hangman   how you envy your children
how you'd reverse polarity so that they'd
be born as dead as you've made yourself
how you'd bind the leather of your heart
tightly over the flesh of theirs
how you'd sew it cold without sweating

       don't you know
       that unbound hearts beat faster
       than yours does?

         don't you know
         they know the games of flight
         that birds in love make?

Elegy of Veil

em morf ta   enog from me
the dnah that had included you
hated evid the upswung dive
mid li ght cut in dim hope
dim glum mid dim exclusiasto
denepo hand held out in evident mist
tsim   cut cold hopish freeze i mraw
warm opened death   flitted horizon   grief
        so to jaw waj   iaw   mai
        maia the sight of slipping away
        dozens of uoy the time seeping
        hold fast   my gnivil friend
        deeper than this eht veil of sraet
        tears be liev this veil gone   enog

Toronto Poem

toronto city between that i lived twice
have want that want you
between oceans like handprint on memory
bloor left on yonge turn there's april snow inside
your toronto of the mind
lean left or right   changes now on king street
mad to read you then   need to read you now
toronto twenty years later you're new again
       toronto you are the toronto of the mind's
       new names   books i remember every apartment
       poets every street left or right
       of bookstore stepped into out of the snows
       of the memory of lost in years the
       walk crunched home and now i am here now

Moos

le t'sst art
le aw ake with th
e cows in theb ranch
es the irs ong
     the hope that
     though they sing
     none of them
     lands on your shoulder
theh opet hough that the ysing
the ru mor sin the moo sic
the mosaic chat terof it so perating sy
stem lou den ough tos
sing the moon
     the quiet   relieved ex
     halations of birds
such moos
to hear it
so lightly
     its vert
     i calm e ado ws

That There Were Other Cities

full orchards are usually useless as motel rooms
seem buried as electricity gods   the station wagons
who usually stayed put   formed downtown witnesses
sue the bastards   see what happens
two hundred seventy-five of them masquerading as easy chairs
knew that the fish came close to serving as a luggage rack
i was there with you father in the old palace
high as the revolutionaries' neon in the town square under our names

    1) emulating fast food was treated with a slow burn
    2) a conflict between earlier years meekly followed
    3) at night use fried chickens as public relations men
    4) serve our customers progress throughout the film
    5) no signs have been destroyed but most people do anyway
    6) every place you go someone's footprints follow you

Railroad Dawn

they've been gathering at the train station four weeks running now
police   carnival barkers   sleep doctors
lawyers with morse code keys attached to their fingers
they're waiting for the large blue egg on the third platform to hatch

every morning just before i wake up it wobbles
there are scratching sounds inside it and all the trains
suddenly get quiet and that's the signal
for the people who have come here to quiet down too

      no one passes judgment on the value of a dawn
      it's new despite itself   it resembles
      itself as it's been over and over again since before the dinosaurs
      but no one arrests its motion   holds it to law
      after all it's only earth turning over in its sleep
      after all when it's done it can't go back to slumber

Motel Room Morning

nothing parallels anything else anywhere
the imagination curves itself around windows
where the glass is furthest in its slow liquid sag
to thickness at the bottom of the frame
distorting the pathos of cars outside the window
their imagined and sad journeys
destinations   too
fictional in the minds of the drivers

    my face is deteriorating
    it's not just the imperfections in the mirror
    or unevenness of light in a motel bathroom
    if there were a diagram or a plan to this it would fall apart too
    cars stalled outside   their horns' notes not parallel or random
    this motel room will be here miles after it's been deserted

You Nork

you nork
bipolar end of an opposite continent
the opposite pull
be able to pull with their own power
forty stories down into your memory
remember their pull from forty years ago
the fire grown solid out of the ground
out of your eyes
       the weakness my knees feel
       even under water   even in the
       imagined heights i walk quickly under
       heights i am   such human heights
       the millions that walk like souls around me
       the other souls too   that walk

Window Street

if i open
window:
street

i   there
a frantic
they

a red car running
carrying
groceries

then who
then no one

lonely window

then i
lifted i
one by one

then
city
i
the city

Freud's Cigar

the heat you engender when you cut deep into the bone
its marrow imaginary as a subterranean river
dream of the voices that have kept you waiting
deep inside the meat of your computer
electrical waterways   passages of zeroes and dots
open socket to a paradise that seems too wet to touch
and a clown's nose at the end of the trail

     congratulations   kid
     you're in heaven

painted on the inside of your eye is an image of the empire state building
in thirty or so years it'll have been there a century
it's still in front of your eyeball when you sleep
as you walk your leggy poodle round and round it
which leg   the dog sniffs   which leg to use
everything's a fire hydrant sometimes
and the butcher shop's closed
all the loose bones are locked in and safe
so which leg to lift now
which leg to lift

Midtown Ride

two nights ago i was ahead of myself
the woman   lake like a horizon
to my left was guiding spirits after two years of chaos
had gotten caught just below my left eyebrow

i dreamt i was on a bus
fish had been flying overhead they had a great view
holiday lights and i became myself
looks a little like manhattan up there

      i'm switching guardian spirits after two years
      of what must have been an elaborate passage
      her hooks   whose profile looked a little
      more like mine in the mirror
      i could understand that one
      it was just me outside the window looking back in

East River

just to the east of the east village   beyond the place beyond looking
his cat's sleep is the transition   in its eye the door to
revived itself as a great heap to carry around
afraid to do so the end of a subway ride among the atlantic oceans

i'm exhausted after walking blocks locked away from elegant staircases
i want to check out   be grinding off
and just as certainly toss up love to the windows
as in the village there's a murmured life of printed halitosis

    i look into eyes   materials
    all of whom grown up and they just flush away
    to see into other eyes   more distant   magazines this time
    the ship heading inland pulling an ocean
    i can feel it crawling up the skin of the statue of liberty
    eyes lined at it across the harbor like a herd of art

National Flags

bankers   in love with an apple
losing their hats to a breeze on the fortieth floor of their bald spots
still   not a hard time

anacondas   back street shoe leather
volcanic pebbles gathered around a fire hydrant of suspense
filming an elbow that's in flames

traffic passes over the roof like pachyderms in a circus tent
smoke is a natural condition of the lungs
smog one of the heart
every curse i curse i curse for you o city of my dreams
i dream you in my sleep
i've got you that memorized
otherwise you'd be a vacant lot for me

     the origin of national flags
     in the feet of small flightless birds
     performing the same urban ritual five days a week

     swimming tar beach
     my don't the clouds look relaxed today
     must be doing the backstroke

sidewalks are the graveyards of centuries of footprints
generations of elephants all out for the same slice of pie
subway tubes evolved in your lungs even in summer rush hour

     old comic book
     half a century later
     the latter-day key
     the latter-day bus
     they're all still out there waving
     cheering in a language we both speak

Subway Ride to the Village

so we took that   a train back
the window glass to remember explanations
so the subway   the way up from down
the din and the clash of streets defined by love

car seat of dream   the ocean its own beach
lest i knew the twentieth century
large romantic man in his forties singing love songs from car to car
best museum in new york

>   god and his characters
>   let's try that one again now
>   a subway ride where they'd never considered it
>   remove the tape from the package
>   i'll have sparrows in my ears
>   and a new pastrami sandwich and egg cream for you

Fast as a New York Sonnet

down this horizonless sidewalk of coffee
the buildings are supported by the doors of coffeehouses
the sidewalk runs as fast as caffeine will carry it
each step each stride each dance step its very own

some day   some say
the free music will end and you'll have to pay the piper
for all the shoe soles you've worn out on these walks
but you'll only have to teach the piper a new tune

    noah's ark landed in washington square park
    it landed there over and over again
    at least every five or ten years it landed
    but lots of times it rains and washes the old footprints away
    people forget about that even with coffee
    that's why this place is so wonderful

Sketch

every time i run around the corner
i find footprints in the concrete where i've been
but i keep running   it's my purpose in life
and the footprints keep following me

somebody offered me myself on a popsicle stick
with a rope around my neck
now i run with myself hanging over my chest
and i'm never lonely

> sit sagging in my armchair   charcoal in my hand
> making marks on a piece of used paper
> until the marks each get up and run away
> walk around the corner   over the footprints
> this is good   it makes the paper empty
> i can sit here   making marks   forever

Architectural

earlier   other lifetime
the tour of the old house headache
the apotheosis of heartburn
to where the soul meets the ceiling

which faced the lacy windows at the edge of
a dome like no other rising straight out of the floor
two aspects of a wall calling back
you breathe the air you have aspirations

      saw a young heavyset blue guitar
      behind a young brunette to be a genius
      we were all nineteen then
      its imagination of little streets
      quietly singing and then asking for money

      oh which path on the wall did we follow?

Looking for Gods in Greenwich Village

i   re   your voice
your that   that beyond
octurnal   thrall   mage
your ear is not your own

runs again in the feet of skyscrapers
i hate looking empty
october   october
it's really octobats

hello i'd like the black sky of sleep
the bookstore was clouds
the first time i went down to the liar death
it's the loneliness there
jugs empty at the fountain of nostalgia
and he finally fell clockface
thought he was a stark can of wood
pressed the light

fishing for muses i saw you
for the hangman's glass walls of the diner
full of wheel   sharp the door
bright of clothing thirty-seven years
as they cross king street
where the hair still almost yellow
o hangman   how i say to you
how you'd revise my coffee
be born dead as silly
tightly over the flesh of table
and after that any surprise
how you'd sew it
such moos

here i go all over town
and i really feel lost without it
the heat you engender when i was ahead of myself
its marrow imaginary as a lake like a horizon
dream of the voices   day on a bus
flying overhead   they had a great view
and a clown's nose like mine in the mirror

the centaur is both human and equine
past and now   leaving
shoeprints below the sidewalk as it moves
you walk that way too
so much space between heart-pounding
and all those loose bones are looking loose
i become oneself   like manhattan up there
love me two times   girl
and like myth   you're in heaven
just to the east of the east village
eyes lined at the feet of small flightless birds
i'll have sparrows in my ears
making marks forever

Aunted

thes amet ime
ha da visi on:
ah aunted
thi ckness
an dat rapdo or
   hi ding
the reis so meg hostly
du ring then ight

Train Station

the whole night in a circle of starlight
passports weren't even checked
      three centuries turned into a railroad car
      that runs the black expanse
      of five hours' choreographed sleep
      as the dead awoke and a fight began
      between two facing seats in the dining car
i boarded the train to the end of the station
      i kissed the doors of a stradivarius violin
      i talked with two drunken cigars
      i spent hours discussing plane geometry
      with the contours of fellow passengers' brains
      watching the ice-capped peaks
      of the sailing ships as they drifted by
even though i'm not in love with melancholy anymore
      they'd named it the street of the train station
      even though its course bordered the lake
      that swallowed the sun   by night
      and spent the morning trying to find its reflection
      the castles   the theaters
      the entire opera i'd made up for both of us
      shimmered upside down in the wisdom of
      the lake's apparent emptiness
      i kissed the doors of la scala for you
      and tasted   sweet   lake water

Mem Mo

o mento
o month a short time
rue teen o aft or
that fifty years have passed
that light   o   fair
by flash   once
springs   a time when
o mento gone
      whee o mento gone
      age whuh so mo
      mento gone old so
      no so old o go
      ne synapse o
      na   so old   gone

Telegraph Avenue Relic

i've walked down this street so many times
that they've set sidewalks over my footprints

even the pavement
is more transient than i am

i remember languages these buildings used to speak
in the stone ages before this century
hello black cat on the psychedelic poster
your green eyes are still following me in their madness
as old buildings resurrect across your path
and i continue my conversations with you

ohlone earth   vaquero earth
student earth for over a century
all these earths would touch the soles of my shoes
if i could step through
the layers of footprints people have put down
beyond the fewer than seventy years
of my own

Borrowed End

tell me when i'm fog   and
almost established as a physical logger-shirted grandfather
walking the whole street's ethereal liquids
on a leash down telegraph avenue
      into the mirror brushed up against itself
      over and over into what you'd guess to be infinity
      one image for each year   all the years you've wandered
      the park still asleep in its delusion and the only light
      a candle settled on a borrowed end table
      that's been in this house since the 1890's

be a long night   duffle bag over his shoulder
and you can decant a noir movie or a nineteenth century
and its lethal fogs   hey sailor   long decade this night
with the killer lawn gnome on this northbound bus
the hippie sidewalks   punk traffic lanes
center line in the night's invisibility of blacktop
my fingers still walk warhol's new york city
as the bus goes further into temporal inscrutability
and cars blur around memory a familiar fog
      in the mirror there you can see the legends
      getting smaller no matter how well you
      remember them in the candle light
            is that a tie dye or a toga
            a periwig or do they know
            how to cure and dye animal skins yet
                  this new borrowed time's in his duffle too
                  as the warm light flows his course
                  across the range of the mirror

Just Across the Water

the laundry blesses you as it hangs across the torch
then disappear   we live table
constant   of light   a city larger within him
all those little figures of small decisions
the soul its own trophy

dnah dnah dnah   tsim
warm opened   no one arrests its motion
beyond the place   beyond its eye
if i could step hguorht
resurrect across your path

the full filed teeth of your little crackling
the apartments inside you opened
flooded in sheer hilarity
        you have taken a long and beautiful tune
        the irregular heave against philosophical neuroses
        magnetizing the force of district
        both small   and large as a footprint
        tnirptoof
the deep city jostle a living bumpy floor
a citywide but glass and steel
a grace of earth   below skyline
the footsteps of cloud's childhood

Looking for Your Brother Again

the kitchen door open someone recognized it as a room
brief there   reptilian big show   heartbeat
his ribcage which had been interrupted
he was whittling a place down the hill
shaping it in his shoulders
forcing a smile
which he left dry every time he worried

> this was remorse
> this is how the novel
> was supposed to begin

but he has a brother left in his head
jugs empty at the fountain of nostalgia
talking a whole era as prescription
he opened the door   and his own light met him
he barked   at last recognizing napoleon's ghost
a stranger turning out to be a cliché in eagle feathers

> a quiver of arrows brought him a rope
> out of the quicksand the rank reek of heroism
> hell   at least you found the sight of light
> that shadow was your brother

hope standing prostitute against a blank wall
the heaving death of boarded-up buildings
from now on   he decided   dead horses
invite them in   turn a statue into a doctor
so you could see him do it   ha
so he could send you smiling
and this   is how the novel ends

Deserts Under Water

the full filed teeth of your little rubber sailors
skateboarding
across floors scarred by centuries of memory

    the apartments inside your eye
    flooded in the sheer hilarity
    of the laughter shared between their walls

you have taken a long and beautiful look
across a deep desert of oceans
elizabethan high beds surfing across a living bumpy floor
the soulful lassitude and drama
of underwater lights of broadway

    the irregular heave against glass and steel
    by the random currents of extrapolated vision

    medical plantlife on the top floor of the clouds
    magnetizing the force of their seeds at ground level

    the swaying grasses of the grace of vacant lots
    that grow as eyebrows of earth below skyline

    your memory of these places
    both small and large as the footsteps of childhood

no matter
children still play here
sing
    we live here
    we live here
    our songs and our games
    are alive here

Backstage at the Met

let me show you the backdrop for my opera:
        the headlights of a car
        half buried in mud
        its death agony shortly thereafter
and the characters
nobody has to invent them:
        soaked and misty soprano
                you clearly   we were all such time
        tenor open at the throat
                i am here   no reason
                that's why that's it
basses accepting fivers
        maybe dimes or living quarters
winged by potential   all the other cast members
        buried tones   alt low
        mezzo standing in the middle
a black sky energy face of the stars speaks
if you can't sing just hum the lines

the blood of the alley entire
the deep city avenues of your imagination
the orchestra of individual car horns
your opera free in the street of the streets
rabbits that leap in their ecstasy on sidewalks
a citywide burst of theatre fronts and sixty-story exuberance
throughout this opera you are still singing amazing me
all these footprints   startled genetics remembering your face
your phantom disrobed and filled to the soul
the soul visible   the physical purification of energy

Hearts of Light

sWOllEn hearts weep
then sleep

all that gLITters seems bRIGHT
in **DARK OF NIGHT**

aWAKENed at soME wee hour
rain makes a **NEW FACE** at the window
then erases it
THEn an**OTHER NEW** one
all for new eyes
until the **WINDOW**
SMILES BACK

wINdow **FACES MAKE LIGHT**
from streetlights

ALL that **HAPPINESS**
HIGHer than streetlight
from that height
FLOWS
down
TO EARTH

For Judy

sitting propped up   against a tooth
in a forest of deciduous rainstorms
i hold your moon in my hands
        like an archaeopteryx
        like a model of the town of ur
        like a blue mushroom's urgent dreams of sunrise
sweat drops   from leaves
footprints erase themselves around me
a lake   far away
takes its place among the clouds
        and your moon glows like a heart
        and i try to find songs for it
        and the tooth is so smooth
        the ground below it so warm
        that it sighs in the moonlight

Reminds Me of Sleepy and a Place to Bury Yourself In

mouth   open ear   tympani
in their music the crackling even the upstairs of the street
the dumped   the abandoned   the begiggled
the grizzled automata their singing grown to garbage can level
song of lost teeth   tone of tattered accompaniment
code's other door opened   no dealer card visible

the shy   agony   of light
the dawned men up from the sidewalk
prostitutes of fortune   creatures of bow and arrow
animal feed aimed at everybody's mouth
it gets that way sometimes
use these sunglasses to visit our carnival
i can hear a ritual desert approaching

reminds me of geophysical neurosis and
growing up a short distance
a frantic grandfather's house
a short-handled meal to anyone who looks
they've done the district and it looks like a young woman i once knew
the first time i saw it it just stopped   winked
nowhere near as fine as peasants being restored
reminds me of very little half a block ago
echo code door opened
that short sharp noise again
reminds me of a footprint my dog found in pompeii
the whole district discovering the power
when everybody puts their forefingers together
and hums

Free

In a hot kITCHen
CATch the fASt ketchup
beFoRE thE cat's
BrEAkfaST

awaKENness runs
inTOdaY's childhood's
WONDER

Credits

Several of the poems in this collection have appeared in the following publications:

"Armweary Traveler," "Two Kids Playing Catch," "The Hangman's Beautiful Children," "Exchange," "National Flags," and "Pomp and Circumstance" appeared in *Transcendent Visions.*

"Moos" appeared in *Ambush Review.*

"Railroad Dawn" appeared in *The Crazy Child Scribbler.*

"Freud's Cigar" appeared in *Bay Area Poets Seasonal Review.*

"Aunted" appeared in *Lost and Found Times.*

"Free" appeared in *Tip of the Knife.*

"Telegraph Avenue Relic" appeared in "Dale Jensen's Poetry Page," an online blog.

Acknowledgments

Thanks to Judy Wells, Melinda Wells Kavanagh, Nancy Wells Brewer, and Melvin Wells for the title of this book.

Thanks to Grace Grafton, John Rowe, Crag Hill and Jack Foley, for their kind words on the frontispiece.

Thanks to David Balmer of New York for use of his art. Balmer is a transplanted South African/Australian painter who now makes his home in the Big Apple.

Thanks to Margaret Copeland of Terragrafix and to Minuteman Press, both of Berkeley, California, for their expertise in handling the production and printing of *Yew Nork*.

And, thanks to Jannie M. Dresser of Sugartown Publishing for her advice, knowledge, and help in producing this book.

About the Author

Dale Jensen was born in Oakland, California, graduated from the University of California at Berkeley in 1971, and received a master's degree in experimental psychology from the University of Toronto in 1973, with which he said goodbye to academia forever. In 1974, he embarked on a career with Social Security that lasted until 1999, when he took early retirement. He lives in Berkeley and is married to the poet Judy Wells.

Dale's poetry is heavily influenced by the Surrealists and such cut-up writers as Bob Cobbing, William Burroughs, and Brion Gysin and has appeared in *Talisman, Lost and Found Times, Ur-Vox, Poetry East, Inkblot, Convolvulus, Dirigible,* and other publications. He edited and published the experimental poetry magazine *Malthus* from 1986 through 1989 and continues to occasionally publish books through Malthus Press. He also has published six books and three chapbooks of poetry: *Thebes* (1991), *Bar Room Ballads* (1992), *The Troubles* (1993), *Twisted History* (1999), *Purgatorial* (2004), *Cyclone Fence* (2007), *Oedipus' First Lover* (2009) and *Auto Bio* (2010).

Thee do I crave co-partner in that verse
Which I presume on Nature to compose...
Divine one, give my words
Immortal charm.
    — *Lucretius, 50 BCE, De Rerum Natura*

Sugartown Publishing

Based in Crockett, California, home to the famous C&H Sugar plant.

SUGARTOWN PUBLISHING JOINED A LONG-ESTABLISHED TRADITION OF COOPERATIVE PUBLISHING IN **2012.** We are dedicated to bringing into print, electronic and audio media formats *works of literary merit that have something significant to say.*

Current and forthcoming titles include:

A Stalwart Bends, Poems and Reflections, by Ben Slomoff (2012).
Doing Time With Nehru, memoir by Yin Marsh (2012).
Among the Shapes that Fold & Fly, poetry by Patricia Nelson (2013).
Between the Fault Lines: Eight East Bay Poets, edited by Jannie M. Dresser (2013).
Workers' Compensation: Poems of Labor & the Working Life, by Jannie M. Dresser (2013).
Swimming the Sky, poetry by Gail Peterson (2013).
It Lasts a Moment: New & Collected Poems, by Fred Ostrander (2013).
Falling Home, poetry by Gary Turchin (2013).
Voices from the Field, poetry by Kimberly Satterfield (2014).
At My Table, poetry by Judith Yamamoto (2014).
The Glass Ship, poems by Judy Wells (2014).
Yew Nork, poetry by Dale Jensen (2014).

Contact us for more information on how we can help you get your book into print.

sugartownpublishing.com
janniedres@att.net
Mailing address:
1164 Solano Ave. #140,
Albany, CA 94706

Colophon

The font used in this book is Minion for the headings and text. Minion is a digital typeface designed by Robert Slimbach in 1990 for Adobe Systems. The name comes from the traditional naming system for type sizes, in which minion is between nonpareil and brevier. It is inspired by late Renaissance-era type.